Enjoy This Book!

Manage your library account and discover all we offer by visiting us online at www.nashualibrary.org.

Please return this book on time so others can enjoy it, too.

If you love what your library offers, tell a friend!

@ Nashua Public Library
2 Court Street, Nashua, NH 03060
603-589-4600, www.nashualibrary.org

J

Cyberspace RESEARCH

NASHUA PUBLIC LIBRARY

By Barbara M. Linde

Gareth Stevens
Publishing

Please visit our website, www.garethstevens.com. For a free color catalog of all our high-quality books, call toll free 1-800-542-2595 or fax 1-877-542-2596.

Library of Congress Cataloging-in-Publication Data

Linde, Barbara M.
 Cyberspace research / Barbara M. Linde.
     p. cm. — (Cyberspace survival guide)
 Includes index.
 ISBN 978-1-4339-7217-1 (pbk.)
 ISBN 978-1-4339-7218-8 (6-pack)
 ISBN 978-1-4339-7216-4 (library binding)
 1. Cyberspace—Juvenile literature. 2. Electronic information resources—Juvenile literature. 3. Research—Methodology—Juvenile literature. I. Title.
 ZA4060.L56 2013
 025.04—dc23
                                        2012011385

First Edition

Published in 2013 by
Gareth Stevens Publishing
111 East 14th Street, Suite 349
New York, NY 10003

Copyright © 2013 Gareth Stevens Publishing

Designer: Katelyn E. Reynolds
Editor: Therese M. Shea

Photo credits: Cover, p. 1 Catalin Petolea/Shutterstock.com; pp. 1, 3–24 (background) Gala/Shutterstock.com; cover, pp. 1, 3–24 (grunge banner; cursor graphics; search box graphic) Amgun/Shutterstock.com; pp. 4, 17 (main image), 27, 28 iStockphoto/Thinkstock.com; pp. 5, 7, 20 Lisa F. Young/Shutterstock.com; p. 9 Alexander Hassenstein/Getty Images; p. 10 Hemera/Thinkstock.com; p. 13 Jupiterimages/Brand X Pictures/Getty Images; pp. 14, 24 Nicholas Kamm/AFP/Getty Images; p. 15 ©iStockphoto.com/youngvet; p. 17 (screen image) Vivan Mehra/The India Today Group/Getty Images; pp. 19, 25 ©iStockphoto.com/cruphoto; p. 23 Creatas Images/Thinkstock.com.

Printed in the United States of America

CPSIA compliance information: Batch #CS12GS: For further information contact Gareth Stevens, New York, New York at 1-800-542-2595.

CONTENTS

Words in the glossary appear in **bold** type the first time they are used in the text.

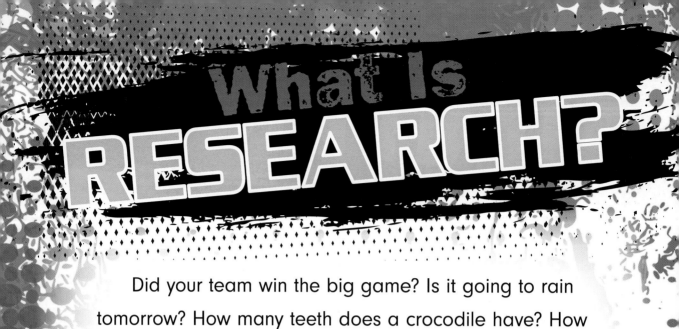

What Is RESEARCH?

Did your team win the big game? Is it going to rain tomorrow? How many teeth does a crocodile have? How did the Internet begin? Whenever you look for answers to questions like these, you're doing **research**.

When you conduct research, you collect facts about a subject. You may read books, magazines, encyclopedias, or newspapers. You may interview experts, watch TV shows or movies, or use your own experiences. And if you're like millions of other curious people today, your research will take you to cyberspace. But cyberspace is a big place, so it's important to know how to get around.

The word "cyberspace" was made up by William Gibson, a science fiction writer. He began using the word in his stories in 1982. The prefix *cyber-* means "computer." Today, cyberspace is the term used for the Internet and other means of electronic communication.

For school projects, use both books and the Internet to find the most trustworthy and up-to-date research on subjects.

What Is Cyberspace RESEARCH?

Cyberspace isn't really a place, like a neighborhood, state, or country. The word "cyberspace" refers to all the communication and interaction that takes place on the Internet. So what's the Internet? It's an electronic network that connects billions of people all over the world. You can't see it, but you most likely use it or know someone who uses it every day.

The Internet is a powerful tool for helping you conduct research. As with all tools, results are most effective when you use it correctly. Following some basic guidelines will turn you into a capable, intelligent Internet researcher.

When Did It Start?

Today's Internet grew out of a government program that started in 1969. By 1980, many large computers across the country were connected. The public was first able to use the Internet in the early 1990s. By 2011, more than 2 billion people around the world were using the Internet!

Each time you log on to the Internet, think about how many people may be logged on at the same time—about 273 million people in North America alone!

7

The Tools OF THE TRADE

Before you can begin your cyberspace research, it helps to know the names of the main tools you'll use and what they do.

- **World Wide Web** Also called the web, this is the system of linked computers and **information** accessed through the Internet. The web includes text, pictures, audio, and video.

- **Browser** A browser is the program that allows a computer to access the Internet. Firefox, Internet Explorer, Safari, and Google Chrome are browsers.

- **Search Engine** A search engine is a program that searches the web using keywords. It returns a list of websites containing those words. Google, Yahoo!, Ask, and Bing are free search engines.

8

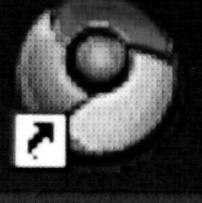

Google Chrome

🔍 Not All for Free

Encyclopedia Britannica Online is also a search engine. You can get some information for free, but there's a fee to use the whole site. The fee may be worth it if you plan to do a lot of research because you know you can trust it as a source. Some other sites also charge.

Mozilla Firefox

Internet Explorer Browser

Each browser has its own icon, or picture, to help you recognize it on a computer screen.

9

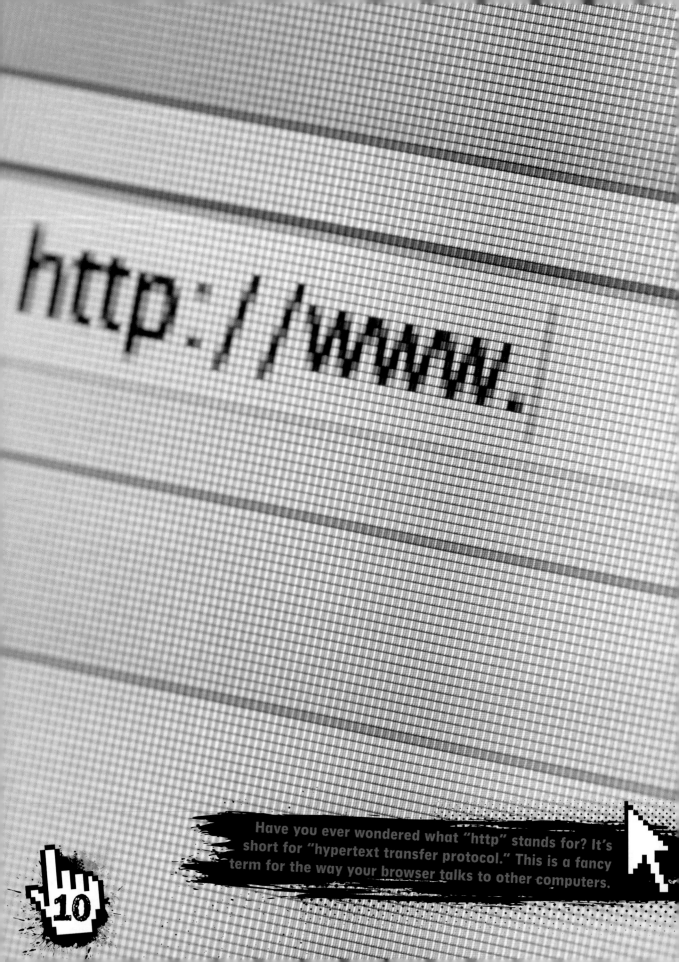

Have you ever wondered what "http" stands for? It's short for "hypertext transfer protocol." This is a fancy term for the way your browser talks to other computers.

10

Website A website is a place on the web. It may be one or more pages and is usually owned or managed by one person, group, or company. Your school might have a website. Zoos, cities, and rock stars have websites. Maybe you have one, too!

URL The URL (Universal Resource Locator) is the address for a website or online **document** or file. Every website has its own address, just like you have a street address. The address starts with the code *http://* or *https://* followed by a name. For example, the URL for the National Zoo in Washington, DC, is *http://nationalzoo.si.edu.*

🔍 Thanks, Sir Tim!

Sir Tim Berners-Lee invented the World Wide Web and the way we access the information on other computers. It first came into use on the Internet in 1991. He offered the use of the web for free, so anyone could use it. By the year 2000, about 360 million people all over the world used the web.

11

Ready, Set, SEARCH!

How do you start your cyberspace research? First, think about what you need to find out. Then, make a list of keywords. You'll need these for your search engine.

Suppose you want to research kangaroos. You can put the word "kangaroo" at the top of your word list. What exactly do you want to know? If you want to find out more about where they live, you could add "Australia." If you want to know about their pouches or their babies, add those words.

Here's a sample search word list:

🔍 Kangaroo Keywords

- kangaroo
- Australia
- pouch
- baby

Spell It ~~Write~~ Right!

Spelling counts when you do a search. If you misspell a word, you might not get the right results. If you're not sure how to spell a word, check a dictionary or ask someone for help. Some search engines make suggestions about how to correctly spell a word.

Sometimes you have to read a bit about your subject before you do your research. You'll find better keywords to use in your online search.

13

Start Your ENGINE!

After you decide what you want to research, open your browser. Type the name of a search engine into the address bar. Let's say you want to use the Google search engine. Enter the URL *www.google.com*. The *http://* will appear once you hit "enter."

The search engine's **homepage** will come up on your screen. You'll see an empty box near a search button. Type "kangaroo" in the box, and then click on the Google Search button.

Most browsers provide easy access to one or more search engines. You might find a search box, or bar, at the top of the screen when you open a browser.

Article   Discussion

Read   Edit

Web search engine

From Wikipedia, the free encyclopedia

(Redirected from Search engine)

"Search engine" redirects

A **web search engine** is

IKIPEDIA

ree Encyclopedia

page

tents

tured content

Just for Kids!

Different search engines might take you to different websites. If you don't like the results you get with one search engine, try another one. Ask Kids at *www.askkids.com* and Yahoo! Kids at *kids.yahoo.com* are specially made for young people. Your school might also have a special search engine you can use.

Web   **Images**   News

Ask

bing

Images

Google

Web   Images   Videos   Maps   News   Shopping   Gmail   more

Web   Images

YAHOO!®

Yahoo!   Make Y! your homepa

YAHOO! SITES   Edit

Mail

Autos

Dating

Finance (Dow Jones)

When researching, try several different search engines. They all search differently and will produce different results. Try it out yourself.

Google

Jobs

15

So Many CHOICES!

Yikes! Now your screen is filled with websites about kangaroos. How do you know which ones to choose? First, scroll, or move the text down the page. Read the title and **description** of each website.

You see that one entry is called "The Pantry." When you read the description, you find out that this site is for a business that has the word "kangaroo" in its title, not about the animal. You know that's not a good site for your research. However, you have several promising **hits**, so it looks like your first keyword was a success.

🔍 The First, but the Best?

Wikipedia is an online encyclopedia. It often comes up first during a search, but that doesn't mean it's the best source. Anyone can write or change an entry, so the information might not be **reliable**. Many teachers won't let students use Wikipedia as a source. Be sure to check with your teacher before you do.

If you can't see a good site to use in the first 30 or so hits, you'll need to try different keywords.

Clues in the ADDRESS

The URL of a website gives you a lot of useful information. The first part, *http://*, is a code that helps browsers read sites on the Internet.

The middle part is the **domain name**. This is the address of the person, business, or organization. It tells other computers how to locate the information.

The last letters in the domain name are called the domain extension. They're a clue about where the information comes from. This chart shows some common domain extensions.

Domain Extension	Type of Information
.com	business
.edu	schools, education
.gov	government
.mil	military
.net	network, business
.org	organization

You might know someone else who has the same name you do. No two domain names are alike. Anyone who wants a domain name has to register online at a domain name website. They can search for the name they want on a list of URLs. If it's in use, they have to think of another name.

Wikipedia is a not-for-profit organization, so it has the domain extension *.org*.

Many schools and libraries have special services that help with research. Ask your librarian.

If you know the domain name, you can make decisions about the quality of the website's information. Look at this URL from your search for facts about kangaroos:

www.kidsplanet.org/factsheets/kangaroo.html

The domain name is kidsplanet. Right away, you can tell the website is meant for kids and probably deals with science subjects. The *.org* extension tells us the site is an organization, not a business. That means it's most likely interested in sharing information, not selling a product.

The rest of the URL is a path within the website. A folder called */factsheets/* is part of the website, and *kangaroo* is a folder within that folder.

🔍 Country Codes

Many URLs have a country code as part of the domain address. So if you want information about kangaroos, it might be good to look at some websites from their native country—Australia!

.us = United States
.au = Australia
.uk = United Kingdom
.cn = China
.jp = Japan
.mx = Mexico
.ca = Canada

Right SITE

Just as with print books, you have to make sure a website's information is reliable. It should be up to date, too. Usually, sites with *.edu* and *.gov* extensions are written by people whose facts can be trusted. Many *.org* sites are trustworthy, too.

Since anyone can have a *.com* website, double-check the information by looking at other sites. Sometimes, if you scroll all the way down the page, you'll see the site creator's name, the date it was created, and the date it was last updated. These are more clues. For instance, a *.com* site written by Sir Tim Berners-Lee about the web can be considered reliable.

🔍 The Minus Sign

Many search engines, including Bing and Google, let you use the minus sign (or a dash) to cut words out of a search. So typing "-zoo" in a search bar with "kangaroo" means that no search result will include the word "zoo." This is helpful, for example, if you only want to read about kangaroos in the wild.

Even if a site is reliable, if it was last updated in 2000, the information probably isn't up to date.

23

Powerful QUOTES

Putting words in quotation marks in a search bar means that the search engine will look for all the words in that exact order. If you put the words "red" and "kangaroo" in a search bar without quotation marks, the results will include all sites with those words, even if they aren't about red kangaroos. You might get a site about a gray kangaroo with a red apple.

Try the search again with "red kangaroo" together in quotes, and you'll only get sites with the words in that order—next to each other. You'll find a good site about red kangaroos much faster.

MSN | Advanced Search

Advanced Search

Many search engines offer an "advanced search." Usually you click on an advanced search button first. Next, you'll see many boxes to fill to help **refine** your search. You don't have to fill them all in. You can get to a successful result much quicker using this kind of search.

| Web | Images | Videos | Shopp

bing™

◉ Show all   ◉ Only English   ◉ O

Hop on a HYPERLINK

Once you're on a website, you may find certain words are underlined or shown in a different color. This probably means the word is a **hyperlink**. When you click on the word, you move away from the text you were reading, onto another part of the page, or even to another website. The hyperlinks might be in the text, or they may be along the top, bottom, or side of the page. Text with hyperlinks might look like this:

> Kangaroos live mostly in <u>Australia</u>. They belong to a group of mammals known as <u>marsupials</u>.

If you click on "Australia," a new page about Australia will likely pop up on your screen. The same thing will happen if you click on the hyperlink for "marsupials." Check to see if the URL has changed and if you can still trust the site.

Photos and More!

The web is loaded with photos, pictures, and videos. You could watch a YouTube video of a kangaroo hopping around as part of your research. Or you could add images to your report. Some websites charge for use of their pictures. Others, such as *www.pics4learning.com*, will let you **download** and copy images for free.

Some hyperlinks are only noticeable when you place your mouse's cursor, or marker, over the word. The text may turn color or become underlined.

27

cite RIGHT

You must **cite** your cyberspace sources in your research paper. Include the name of the website, the date you got the information, and the URL. Include the author's name if you can.

It's tempting to copy and paste sentences or paragraphs from a website right into your report. DON'T DO IT! That's called **plagiarism**, and it's stealing. Instead, write your own summary. You can quote an author's work if you give the author credit in the text.

So, the next time someone asks you how many teeth a crocodile has or when Paul Revere took his famous ride, you'll know how to research the answer. Head for cyberspace!

The Cyberspace Research Checklist

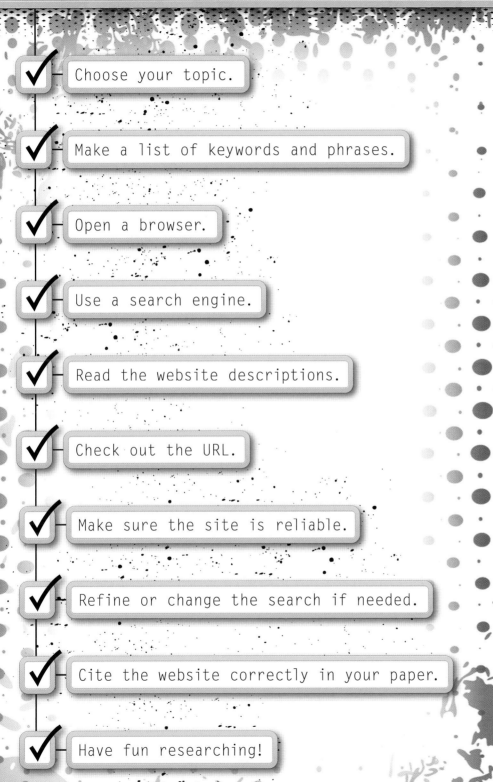

- ✓ Choose your topic.
- ✓ Make a list of keywords and phrases.
- ✓ Open a browser.
- ✓ Use a search engine.
- ✓ Read the website descriptions.
- ✓ Check out the URL.
- ✓ Make sure the site is reliable.
- ✓ Refine or change the search if needed.
- ✓ Cite the website correctly in your paper.
- ✓ Have fun researching!

29

GLOSSARY

cite: to give facts about a source of information, such as title, name of author, and date

description: facts that tell what something is like

document: a computer file created using a program

domain name: a series of characters that identifies a group of online resources and forms part of the URL for the resources

download: to transfer or copy files from one computer to another, or from the Internet to a computer

hit: a result of an Internet search

homepage: the main page of a website

hyperlink: a word, symbol, or image on a website that links directly to another part of the website or to another site

information: facts and knowledge

plagiarism: the act of taking the ideas or words of someone else and pretending they are one's own

refine: to improve something by making small changes

reliable: able to be trusted to be correct

research: the collecting of information to learn more about a topic

For More INFORMATION

Books

Barker, Donald, et al. *Internet Research–Illustrated*. Boston, MA: Cengage, 2011.

Gaines, Ann. *Ace Your Internet Research*. Berkeley Heights, NJ: Enslow Publishers, 2009.

Gerber, Larry. *Cited! Identifying Credible Information Online*. New York, NY: Rosen Central, 2010.

Websites

Answers for Young People
www.w3.org/People/Berners-Lee/Kids.html
Tim Berners-Lee answers questions about how we surf the web.

Tips to Effective Internet Searching
hanlib.sou.edu/searchtools/searchtips.html
Twelve great tips for finding what you need on the web.

INDEX